My Hindu Life

Dilip Kadodwala and Sharon Chhapi

HODDER
Wayland

LOOKING AT RELIGION

My Buddhist Life
My Christian Life
My Hindu Life
My Jewish Life
My Muslim Life
My Sikh Life

For more information on this series and other Hodder Wayland titles, go to www.hodderwayland.co.uk

Editor: Ruth Raudsepp
Designer: Joyce Chester

First published in Great Britain in 1996 by Wayland Publishers Ltd under the series title 'Everyday Religion'
This edition published in 2006 by Hodder Wayland, an imprint of Hodder Children's Books

Hodder Children's Books, a division of Hodder Headline Limited,
338 Euston Road, London NW1 3BH

ISBN-10: 0 7502 4958 7
ISBN-13: 978 0 7502 4958 4

Picture acknowledgements
The author and publishers thank the following for taking photographs and for giving permission to reproduce photographs: Andes Press Agency 14; Axiom Photographic Agency 7, 24; Cephas 13; Chapel Studios 27, *title page*; Circa Photo Library 9; Rupert Horrox 10, *front cover*; Hutchinson Library 15, 16, 19; Impact 27; Panos pictures 23; Ann & Bury Peerless 18, 21, 26; David Rose 4, 5, 8, 11, 12, 17, 18, 20, 22, 25.

Typeset by Joyce Chester
Printed in China

Contents

Jasmine and Viren are Hindus.
Many Hindus start the day with
a prayer.

Hindus say this prayer every morning. It is called the Gayatri Mantra.

Hindus believe there is one God, but that God has many forms. A Hindu chooses one or more of these forms to worship. Here you can see the goddess **Lakshmi**.

When Hindus worship they light a small lamp called a **diva**. This light helps Hindus to think about God. Here the **priest** is sharing water that has been blessed by God.

When Jasmine and her mother enter
a Hindu temple they ring a bell.
This helps them to think about God.
The temple is called a **mandir**.

In the mandir there is a special ceremony called **arti**. The priest holds up five diva lamps and a special prayer is sung.

A Hindu baby's first visit outside the home is to the mandir. At the mandir the baby is blessed.

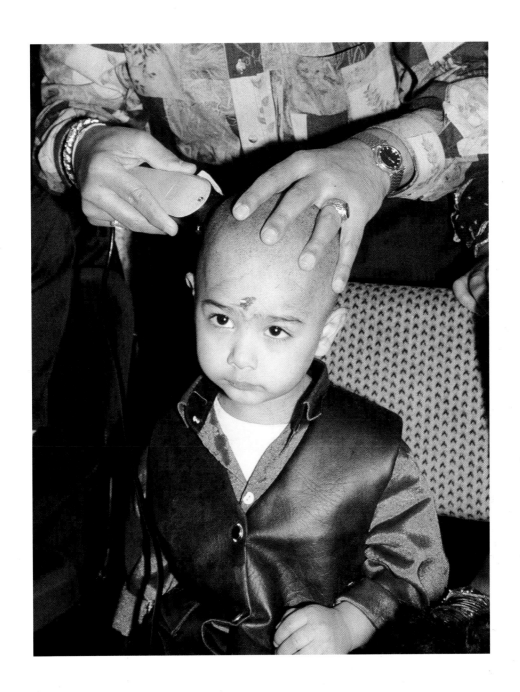

After their first birthday, some Hindu children have their hair cut. The red tilaka mark on the boy's forehead is made by the priest as a way of blessing.

On her wedding day a Hindu bride looks very beautiful. After the wedding is over she will live with her husband's family.

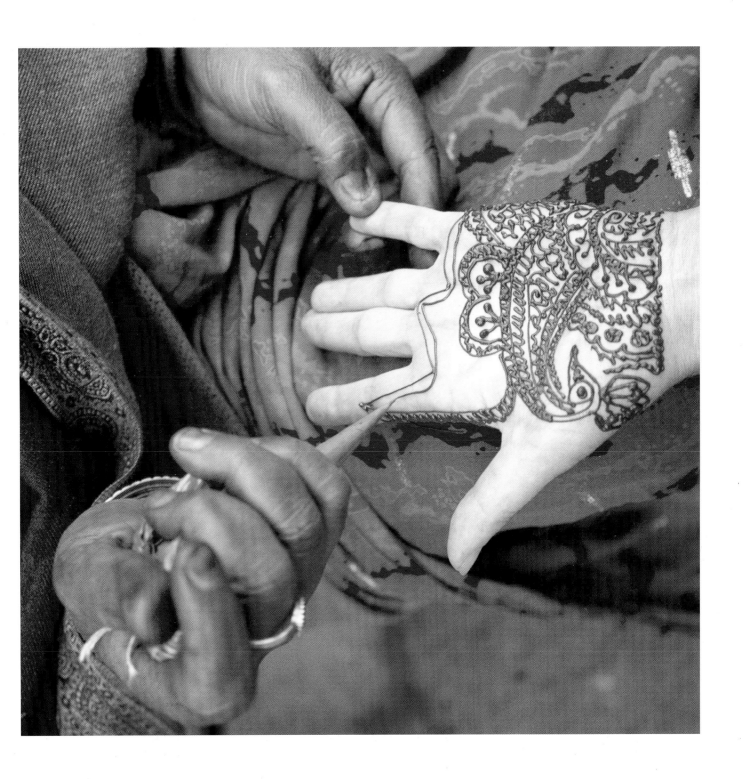

The night before a wedding, the bride's hands and feet are decorated with **henna**.

A Hindu wedding is a special religious time. A lot of families and friends are invited. For children it is a time for meeting up with relatives and having fun.

Weddings are celebrated with a feast. Sometimes in India a rich family will invite all the villagers to the wedding feast.

When a Hindu dies the body is decorated and **cremated**. The ashes are then put into a river and carried away on the water.

Hindus remember someone who has died by putting beads or flowers around their photograph. Some families have a special meal every year on the day that the person died.

Stories of gods and goddesses are read out by a priest, especially during festival times.

Dance and drama are often used to tell the stories of gods and goddesses.

Jasmine shows her love for her brother by tying a **rakhi** on his wrist. Viren gives Jasmine a present and promises to look after her.

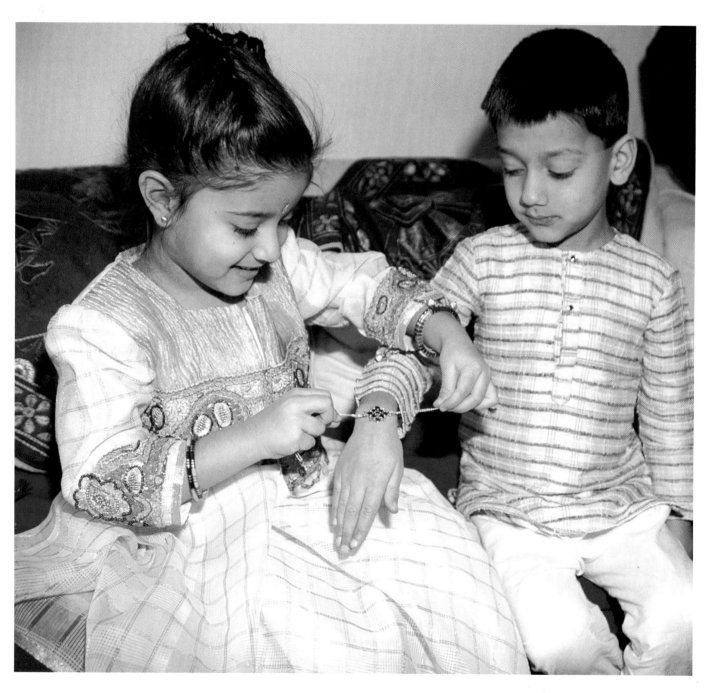

This man is dressed as the evil King Ravana. During the festival of Dusshera a huge model of King Ravana is burned. Hindus believe that good always wins over evil.

During the festival of Diwali Hindus put a pattern on their doorsteps. This pattern, which is made from coloured rice-flour, is called rangoli.

The spring festival of Holi is enjoyed by all Hindu children. They throw coloured powders at each other without being told off!

Hindus believe that all life is holy, and many Hindus do not eat meat. Cows are especially holy, because they are linked with the god **Krishna**.

Special food called **prashad** is offered to God during worship and festivals. The food is then shared with everybody.

 This sign is called aum. It is the Hindu sign or word for God and is said at the start and end of all prayers.

Hindus believe that the whole world is one big family. Everyone should look after each other.

Notes for Teachers

Pages 4 & 5 Prayer is important to Hindus. The act of worship is called 'puja' and it can be performed in the home or temple (mandir). Hindus venerate the One Supreme Being, Brahman. It is believed that God is everywhere and in everything. God is One but has many forms, representing different aspects of the Divine. Sacred Hindu texts came to be written down in Sanskrit, an early form of Indo-Aryan writing. In modern times, texts have been translated into many Indian regional languages. Prayers are mostly in Sanskrit.

Pages 6 & 7 Most Hindu homes have a family shrine. Many families choose a deity or deities as their personal gods. Images in the form of pictures and statues, called murtis, are placed and venerated in the shrine. Sometimes, Hindus think of God as energy which is manifested through three deities called the Trimurti: Brahma, the creator; Vishnu, the preserver and Shiva, the destroyer. Hindus believe that the process of destruction and regeneration is endless. God descends to earth when evil increases, in order to restore goodness. These incarnations of God are called avatars. Devotion is popularly directed towards Shiva and two avatars of Vishnu, namely Rama and Krishna. Male deities are usually accompanied by female aspects of energy, hence there are many important goddesses in the Hindu pantheon.

A diva is twisted cotton wool made into a wick and soaked in clarified butter called ghee. Lighting a diva helps to focus the worshipper's attention on God.

Pages 8 & 9 Hindus believe a mandir is God's abode. When murtis are installed, rituals prescribed in the sacred texts are carefully followed. The culmination of an act of worship in a mandir is the arti ceremony. Five lamps, divas, are lit and placed in a stainless steel tray. The five divas symbolize the elements of nature and the five human senses. Hindus worship with their whole being. The arti tray is circled in front of the deities by the priest, whilst the congregation sing a special hymn. Afterwards, the tray is passed around the worshippers, who take their blessings from God by passing their hands over the flames and drawing their hands over their heads and eyes. Offerings of milk, fruit and sugar crystals are made to the deities and shared by worshippers. This food, blessed by God, is called prashad.

Pages 10 & 11 The Hindu life cycle consists of sixteen traditional steps called samskars. Not all Hindus follow the sacraments linked with the steps. However, most perform the fourth samskar, when a newborn baby is washed and the sacred syllable, aum, is traced on the baby's tongue with honey. The sixth step marks the baby's first outing when she or he is exposed to the health-giving rays of the sun. Many Hindus in the West take the baby to a mandir to be blessed. The eighth step occurs after the first birthday when the baby's hair is shaved off. It symbolizes the removal of bad deeds carried over from previous incarnations and the start of a new life.

Pages 12 & 13 Marriage is a sacred sacrament and a duty. It constitutes the thirteenth of the sixteen steps in the life cycle. Marriage provides an opportunity for Hindu aims and duties to be fulfilled. Preparation before the wedding ceremony includes purchasing a silk sari, jewellery and other clothes for the bride's new life with her husband and his family. The bride's face, hands and feet are painted with henna to enhance her beauty. The intricate patterns made on the palms of the hands is called mehndi.

Pages 14 & 15 Hindu marriages mark the union of the couple and of the two extended families. Great care is taken in matching the qualities and personalities of the marriage partners. Increasingly, the prospective partners have a considerable say in their choice of partners. Hindu weddings can be very large. Men from the bride's side of the family prepare a vegetarian feast. Sometimes the food is prepared by caterers, but it is usually served by male members of the bride's family.

Pages 16 & 17 Hindus believe in reincarnation. The cycle of birth, death and rebirth is called samsara. The ultimate purpose is to be liberated from the cycle.

This liberation is called moksha. To a devout Hindu, the carrying out of religious duties is paramount. Duties and good conduct are referred to as dharma. The word also means 'religion' to Hindus. Good conduct may result in a better life in the cycle of samsara. The accumulation of good and bad deeds is called karma and this defines future existences or the release from the cycle of rebirth. It is the duty of the eldest son to light the funeral pyre, in the hope that the deceased parent will achieve moksha.

A priest performs death rites in the home before the body is taken to a crematorium. Nowadays, many Hindu families send or take the ashes to the River Ganges, a sacred river, where the ashes are scattered. Deceased family members are remembered with a special meal on each anniversary, and a garlanded photo in the home shrine.

Pages 18 & 19 Hindu scriptures are divided into two broad groups, 'revealed' and 'remembered' scriptures. The earliest ones are called the Vedas, meaning knowledge or wisdom. The Vedas comprise of hymns and describe how religious rituals should be conducted. Amongst the 'remembered' texts are the Hindu Epic poems, the Mahabharata (which includes the most popular text, the Bhagavad Gita) and the poem that tells the story of Rama and Sita, the Ramayana. The teachings and stories have been communicated traditionally through dance or theatrical performances.

Pages 20 & 21 Raksha means 'protection' and Bandhan means 'to tie'. The festival celebrates family unity, especially the bond between brothers and sisters. On this day the sister ties a bracelet, called a rakhi, on her brother's right wrist. The rakhi symbolizes the love between brothers and sisters, and is also meant to ward off evil. In turn, a brother promises to protect his sister, and gives her a gift as a token of his love.

The festival of Dusshera celebrates the mother goddess. Festivals are celebrated differently throughout India, but the common thread running through them is the symbolic defeat of evil by the power of God. Burning a huge model of the demon King Ravana is one of the characteristics of the festival of Dusshera.

Pages 22 & 23 A rangoli pattern is a traditional symbol of welcome. It is drawn on a doorstep of a home or mandir. Patterns consist of the sacred syllable aum, and other traditional patterns. Rice-flour and other coloured powders are used to create the patterns. During the festival of Diwali, a rangoli pattern is meant to invite the goddess of good fortune, Lakshmi, to bless a household. The festival of Diwali celebrates the defeat of the demon king Ravana by God incarnated as Rama.

Holi is a spring festival characterized by the lighting of a bonfire, symbolizing the power of good over evil. The story of a boy called Prahlad, who overcomes being destroyed by a fire because of his faith in God, is recalled by Hindus. Holi also commemorates the deity Krishna's youthful pranks. Part of the festival fun for adults and children includes spraying coloured water and dyes over each other.

Pages 24 & 25 Ancient Hindu philosophers described the earth and the universe as the body of God. Hindus believe that all forms of life have souls; this belief results in a reverence for all life forms. Many Hindus do not eat meat, fish or eggs (although this is not observed by all Hindus). The cow is particularly revered because it is linked with Krishna and because of its life-giving properties: milk, butter and dung (used as fertilizer and fuel in parts of India).

Pages 26 & 27 Aum (Om) is a sacred Hindu syllable. It represents the sound of God and creation. The three strands symbolize life, death and rebirth or release. The strands also stand for the three states of consciousness in humans: being awake, dreaming and dreamless sleep. The word is recited at the beginning and at the end of all prayers and worship. Hindus who practise meditation will often chant the word and use it as a focus for concentration during meditation.

The extended family is an important institution for Hindus. It is the means by which religious traditions and wisdom is transmitted across the generations. Hindus regard the world community as a family.

Glossary

arti A special ceremony performed during worship. Five lamps are lit and a special song is sung.

cremated When a Hindu dies their body is burnt and their ashes are scattered on a river.

diva A lamp made out of twisted cotton wool and soaked in melted butter. It is lit when worshipping God.

henna Brown powder from the henna plant is made into a paste, and used to decorate a bride's hands and feet.

Krishna The name of a popular Hindu god.

Lakshmi The Hindu goddess of fortune.

mandir A Hindu place of worship.

prashad Food, such as fruit and nuts, which is blessed by god and then shared with everybody.

priest Someone who performs religious ceremonies.

rakhi A bracelet made from cotton or silk threads.

Further Information

Books to Read

*A Year of Religious Festivals:
My Hindu Year* by Cath Senker
(Hodder Wayland, 2004)

Celebrations!: Divali by Anita Ganeri
(Heinemann, 2004)

Holy Places: The Ganges by Victoria
Parker (Heinemann, 2003)

Our Culture: Hindu by Jenny Wood
(Franklin Watts, 2003)

Places of Worship: Hindu Temples by
Rasamandala Das (Heinemann, 1999)

Talking About My Faith: I am Hindu
by Cath Senker (Franklin Watts, 2005)

The Facts About Hinduism by Alison
Cooper (Hodder Wayland, 2006)

Useful Organisations

Hindu Forum of Britain
Unit 3, 861 Coronation Road,
Park Royal, London
NW10 6PT
Tel: 020 8965 0671
www.hinduforum.org

ISKCON Educational Services
Bhaktivedanta Manor,
Hilfield Lane,
Aldenham,
Watford,
WD2 8EZ
Tel: 01923 859578
www.iskcon.org.uk/ies

The website addresses (URLs) included in
this book were valid at the time of going to
press. However, because of the nature of the
Internet, it is possible that some addresses
may have changed, or sites may have
changed or closed down since publication.
While the authors and Publisher regret any
inconvenience this may cause readers, no
responsibility for any such changes can be
accepted by either the authors or the
Publisher.

Index